YOUR
AUTHOR
BUSINESS PLAN

A Companion
Workbook

TAKE YOUR AUTHOR CAREER
TO THE NEXT LEVEL

Joanna Penn

Your Author Business Plan: Take Your Author Career to the Next Level.
A Companion Workbook.

ISBN: 978-1-913321-56-7

Published by Curl Up Press

Requests to publish work from this book should be sent to:
joanna@TheCreativePenn.com

Cover and Interior Design: JD Smith

Printed by Amazon KDP Print

www.CurlUpPress.com

Contents

Introduction   1
What is a Business Plan?   5

Part 1: Business Summary and Brand   **7**

1.1   Company structure   9
1.2   Business summary and big-picture goals   11
1.3   Author brand   15
1.4   Comparison authors and reader avatar   18

Part 2: Production   **21**

2.1   Products and/or services   23
2.2   Writing process and production schedule   28
2.3   Publishing and licensing strategy   30
2.4   Pricing strategy   32

Part 3: Marketing   **35**

3.1   Strategy. Author ecosystem   37
3.2   Author website   40
3.3   Email list and ARC team   42
3.4   Content marketing   49
3.5   Paid advertising   51
3.6   Social media   54
3.7   Author network   56

Part 4: Financials   **57**

4.1   Money mindset   59
4.2   Revenue model and income   66
4.3   Initial investment and on-going costs   70
4.4   Paying yourself first and long-term investing   74

Your Next Steps   77
Example Business Plans   79
Your Author Business Plan   87
Conclusion 105
Need more help on your author journey?   107

Appendix 1: Resources   109
Appendix 2: Bibliography   113
About Joanna Penn   115

More Books and Courses from Joanna Penn   117

Introduction

You are an author.

You turn ideas into reality in the shape of a book. You turn the thoughts in your head into valuable intellectual property assets. You understand how powerful the written word can be.

This Companion Workbook will help you use your words to create a business plan to take your writing career to the next level — whatever that means for your situation.

* * *

I'm Joanna Penn and in 2009, I created a business plan for what became The Creative Penn Limited, a multi-six-figure company with books at its heart. I'm an award-nominated New York Times and USA Today bestselling thriller and dark fantasy author as J.F. Penn, and I also write non-fiction for authors. I'm an award-winning podcaster with two shows, *The Creative Penn* and *Books and Travel*, and an international professional speaker.

My business has multiple streams of income, including books in different formats in multiple stores, and I've sold copies in 159 countries. I also have online courses, affiliate income, podcast sponsorship and Patreon, among others.

But it wasn't always like this.

I started out with one book, no audience, and no experience in publishing or online sales and marketing. But I wrote a plan for my creative and financial future and took action on my ideas, learning the necessary skills along the way. Since then, I've continued to work toward those original goals and in 2011, I left my corporate job to become a full-time author-entrepreneur. I've never gone back and I love my creative, entrepreneurial life.

* * *

In *Your Author Business Plan*, I guided you through the process of creating a business plan that will help you achieve your creative and financial goals. In this Workbook edition, you will find the questions from each chapter with spaces to write your answers, as well as the example business plans and an area to collate your thoughts.

Your business plan structure

This book follows the structure of the business plan so you can focus on each section in turn as you go through.

Part 1 covers your business summary and author brand, taking you through the process of deciding the overall direction for what you want to achieve and who you want to serve.

Part 2 goes into the production process around your writing, publishing and licensing, products and services.

Part 3 covers your marketing strategy and author ecosystem.

Part 4 goes into the financial side of your business, from mindset to revenue and costs, as well as paying yourself now and into the future.

The final chapter will give you a framework for simplifying your plan and turning it into achievable steps across a chosen timeline.

In each section, I give examples from my own business plan and there are questions for you to answer and resources that might help along the way.

You can find templates and more resources at:

www.TheCreativePenn.com/yourplan

* * *

Note: There are affiliate links within this book to products and services that I recommend and use personally. This means that I receive a small percentage of the sale at no extra cost to you, and in some cases, you may receive a discount for using my link. I only recommend products and services that I believe are great for authors, so I hope you find them useful.

What is a Business Plan?

What is a business plan?

_____

_____

_____

_____

Why do you want to create one for your author business? Why will you spend time on this?

_____

_____

_____

_____

_____

_____

_____

_____

Part 1: Business Summary and Brand

1.1 Company structure

What is your company structure now? What author name/s and/or imprint do you publish?

_____

_____

_____

_____

_____

_____

What would you like your structure to be in the future? What will trigger action on this?

_____

_____

_____

_____

_____

_____

_____

_____

What do you need to research so you're more confident in this area?

1.2 Business summary and big-picture goals

What is your why? Why do you want an author business, anyway?

_____

_____

_____

_____

_____

_____

_____

_____

_____

_____

_____

_____

_____

_____

What is your core life value? Or your top three, if you're struggling with one.

_____

_____

_____

_____

_____

_____

_____

How are you currently living this value? How could you move closer to it?

_____

_____

_____

_____

_____

_____

_____

_____

Who do you serve? Who is your target market?

_____

_____

_____

_____

_____

_____

_____

What will you say "no" to?

_____

_____

_____

_____

_____

_____

_____

_____

_____

What is your business summary, by author brand if applicable?

1.3 Author brand

What is an author brand?

_____

_____

_____

_____

_____

What is your author brand (by author name if that
is applicable)? What is your promise to the reader?
What are the feelings that are associated with it?

_____

_____

_____

_____

_____

_____

_____

_____

_____

_____

What images, colors, and words currently stand out on your book covers and website?

_____

_____

_____

_____

_____

_____

What can you do to make your author brand more recognizable?

_____

_____

_____

_____

_____

_____

_____

_____

_____

_____

_____

Do you have a Brand Manual? Is it time to work with a graphic designer to create one in order to maintain consistency?

_____

_____

_____

_____

_____

_____

_____

_____

_____

_____

_____

_____

_____

_____

_____

_____

_____

1.4 Comparison authors and reader avatar

Who are your comparison authors and what are your comparison books? List by series and author name.

What categories and subcategories are your books in? When was the last time you refreshed these if your books have been out for a while?

_____

_____

_____

_____

_____

_____

_____

_____

_____

_____

_____

_____

_____

_____

_____

_____

What is your reader avatar? By author name and series, if appropriate.

Part 2: Production

2.1 Products and/or services

List your books. Think about series, standalones, novellas, short stories, co-writing, and if appropriate, any articles or papers. Split this out by **author name** if you have multiple brands, or if that's something you're considering. Consider formats, global markets, retailers, languages.

Are you making the most of your possible streams of book income? What specific things will you do in this current plan to expand them?

What other products and/or services do you currently offer? What will you add? What will you stop?

What percentage of your income is time-based,
and what percentage is scalable? Are you happy
with how it is currently? How can you change that?

_____

_____

_____

_____

_____

_____

_____

_____

_____

_____

_____

_____

_____

_____

_____

2.2 Writing process and production schedule

What does your writing process look like right now?

_____

_____

_____

_____

_____

_____

Is it working for you? What could you do to improve it?

_____

_____

_____

_____

_____

_____

_____

Is your writing process sustainable for the long term? What can you do to improve this?

_____

_____

_____

_____

_____

_____

_____

What does your production plan look like for the year ahead?

_____

_____

_____

_____

_____

_____

_____

_____

2.3 Publishing and licensing strategy

For more detail on the practical steps, check out *Successful Self-Publishing: How to Self-Publish and Market Your Book*

How do you currently publish your books? Why did you make this choice? Is there anything you want to improve or change?

What rights do you currently license and what might you explore going forward? What do you need to do to achieve this?

_____

_____

_____

_____

_____

_____

_____

_____

_____

_____

_____

_____

_____

_____

_____

_____

2.4 Pricing strategy

If you have control of your pricing, what is your pricing strategy per genre and format?

_____

_____

_____

_____

_____

_____

Have you adapted these by currency on the relevant stores?

_____

_____

_____

_____

_____

_____

_____

Is there anything you need to change, improve, or experiment with?

_____

_____

_____

_____

_____

_____

_____

_____

_____

_____

_____

_____

_____

_____

_____

Part 3: Marketing

3.1 Strategy. Author ecosystem

What does your author ecosystem look like now?

_____

_____

_____

_____

_____

_____

_____

_____

_____

_____

_____

_____

_____

_____

What do you currently own and control?

_____

_____

_____

_____

_____

_____

_____

If you carry on as you are for the next five years, or ten years, what will your ecosystem look like?

_____

_____

_____

_____

_____

_____

_____

_____

_____

What do you need to change to ensure it works for you over the long term?

_____

_____

_____

_____

_____

_____

_____

_____

_____

_____

_____

_____

_____

_____

_____

_____

3.2 Author website

Do you own and control your author website and/or author domain name? How can you improve this situation?

_____

_____

_____

_____

_____

What is the purpose of your website? Is it serving that purpose?

_____

_____

_____

_____

_____

_____

_____

How does your website drive revenue? Could it be more effective?

_____

_____

_____

_____

_____

_____

_____

Do you need to up-skill in this area or work with someone else to help you?

_____

_____

_____

_____

_____

_____

My tutorial on website hosting, design, and email setup:
www.TheCreativePenn.com/authorwebsite

3.3 Email list and ARC team

Do you currently have an email list of readers? Do you need to set up an email list or split out different brands? Do you have an ARC team?

_____

_____

_____

_____

_____

_____

_____

_____

_____

_____

_____

_____

_____

What service are you using to build and maintain your list? Are you happy with it? Are you adhering to anti-spam and data protection rules? Does your Privacy Policy enable you to use your email list for advertising?

_____

_____

_____

_____

_____

_____

_____

_____

_____

_____

_____

_____

_____

_____

What is your call to action? What are you offering
readers right now?

_____

_____

_____

_____

_____

Do you need to change up your offer?
Do you need to set up or revisit your
autoresponder email sequence?

_____

_____

_____

_____

_____

_____

_____

_____

How are you driving people to your email list so it grows over time? How could you make this more effective?

_____

_____

_____

_____

_____

_____

_____

_____

_____

_____

_____

_____

_____

_____

_____

_____

What is your strategy for emailing in terms of frequency and what do you write about? Are you doing a good job of communicating with your readers?

_____

_____

_____

_____

_____

_____

_____

_____

_____

_____

_____

_____

_____

_____

_____

Are you maintaining your email list and keeping it active? Are you cleaning your list and weeding out unresponsive readers over time?

_____

_____

_____

_____

_____

_____

Which authors in your niche are doing well with email marketing? How could you incorporate some of their best practices?

_____

_____

_____

_____

_____

_____

_____

_____

How could you improve your communication and resulting engagement and sales?

_____

_____

_____

_____

_____

_____

_____

_____

Do you need to up-skill around email marketing?

_____

_____

_____

_____

_____

_____

3.4 Content marketing

What content marketing do you currently produce on your site or others?

_____

_____

_____

_____

_____

What is the point of your content?
How does it attract your target market?
How does it feed into your author ecosystem?
How does it drive revenue?

_____

_____

_____

_____

_____

_____

_____

What would make it more effective? Is there
anything you need to stop doing?

_____

_____

_____

_____

_____

_____

_____

What kind of content marketing do you enjoy
consuming and creating? What suits you and your
audience? What can you sustain for the long term?

_____

_____

_____

_____

_____

_____

_____

3.5 Paid advertising

How are you using paid advertising at the moment? What has worked well before and what has been less effective?

_____

_____

_____

_____

_____

Do you have a schedule for running ads? Do you track your results? How could you be more organized?

_____

_____

_____

_____

_____

_____

_____

What do you need to test or try? How could you improve your paid ads?

How do you feel about paid ads? How will you balance happiness and sales?

3.6 Social media

What social media accounts do you currently have
and how are you using them specifically for your
author business?

_____

_____

_____

_____

_____

_____

How much time and money are you spending
on social media, and is it worth it for your
business goals?

_____

_____

_____

_____

_____

_____

Do you enjoy your social media time? If not, do you really need to continue? How could you make it more sustainable?

_____

_____

_____

_____

_____

_____

_____

_____

_____

_____

_____

_____

_____

_____

_____

_____

_____

3.7 Author network

Do you have an author network already? Is it giving you everything you need?

_____

_____

_____

_____

_____

_____

How could you improve your network? How could you be more active within your chosen groups?

_____

_____

_____

_____

_____

_____

_____

Part 4:
Financials

4.1 Money mindset

What is your current relationship with money? Do you love it, want it, fear it, or something else?

_____

_____

_____

_____

_____

_____

_____

_____

_____

_____

_____

_____

_____

_____

What are the words and phrases that spring to mind when you think about money, maybe from your family, the media, or friends? Are they positive or negative? If you're unsure, can you say out loud, "I love money!"? How does that make you feel?

_____

_____

_____

_____

_____

_____

_____

_____

_____

_____

_____

_____

_____

Are you in control of your current financial situation? Are you actively managing your money?

_____

_____

_____

_____

_____

_____

_____

_____

_____

_____

_____

_____

_____

_____

_____

_____

_____

Have you spent time learning about money? Are you comfortable talking about investments and other aspects of wealth management?

_____

_____

_____

_____

_____

_____

_____

_____

_____

_____

_____

_____

_____

_____

_____

What could you do to improve your attitude to money and your knowledge about how it works?

_____

_____

_____

_____

_____

Do you really want to make money from your books? Are you writing for money or another reason, for example, acceptance, status, sharing your story, or purely for creative reasons?

How much money do you want to make from your
writing in the next year? In the next five years?

_____

_____

_____

_____

_____

_____

_____

What are you willing to do to achieve this
financial goal?

_____

_____

_____

_____

_____

_____

_____

_____

_____

What is your definition of a 'wealthy' author?
Do you want to be a wealthy author?

_____

_____

_____

_____

_____

_____

How do you feel about other writers who are
wealthy? Check out the Forbes Richest Author
List for examples.

_____

_____

_____

_____

_____

_____

List of recommended books and podcasts about money:
www.TheCreativePenn.com/moneybooks

4.2 Revenue model and income

Do you have a separate bank account to manage your author business? Are you tracking income and expenses? Do you know whether you made a profit or a loss in the last period (quarter or year)?

What are your different income streams right now?
How much income do they bring in?

What do you need to stop doing?
What do you need to do more of?

_____

_____

_____

_____

_____

_____

_____

_____

_____

_____

_____

_____

_____

_____

_____

_____

How does each part of your author ecosystem drive revenue for your business? What is working well? What could you improve? Can you justify the parts that don't make money now?

4.3 Initial investment and on-going costs

What initial investment have you made, or do you need to make, in your author business?

_____

_____

_____

_____

_____

_____

How will you fund this initial investment?

_____

_____

_____

_____

_____

_____

What are the ongoing costs for your author business?

Are all these expenses necessary? What are non-negotiable and important for your business? What do you need to reconsider?

_____

_____

_____

_____

_____

_____

_____

_____

_____

_____

_____

_____

_____

_____

_____

_____

How are you tracking your financials? Is there a better option?

_____

_____

_____

_____

_____

_____

_____

What do you need to learn to improve your financial knowledge and management?

_____

_____

_____

_____

_____

_____

_____

_____

_____

4.4 Paying yourself first and long-term investing

Where are you on the stages of the author financial journey?

_____

_____

_____

_____

_____

How can you move to the next stage? How can you increase your income?

_____

_____

_____

_____

_____

_____

_____

Are you paying yourself a salary? Are you currently investing? How can you start or increase both of these?

_____

_____

_____

_____

_____

_____

How confident are you with these financial concepts? What do you need to learn in order to move to the next level?

_____

_____

_____

_____

_____

_____

_____

_____

Your Next Steps

Have you collated and reviewed the relevant material?

_____

_____

_____

_____

_____

Have you simplified your plan as much as possible to ensure it is strategic?

_____

_____

_____

_____

_____

_____

Have you created a separate To Do list or Action Plan with more detailed items?

_____

_____

_____

_____

Have you turned your plan into a timeline and mapped out when you will do the work that's needed?

_____

_____

_____

_____

Have you set a review date on your calendar to revisit and update your plan?

_____

_____

_____

_____

_____

Example Business Plans

Now we've been through all the sections, here are two finished example business plans representing different stages of the author journey. Since I have included details of my advanced business within the book, I've focused this section firstly on a new fiction author and secondly on a more developed non-fiction business.

I have not included answers to the deeper questions, just the basic plan and a few action points so you can see how the process might work for your situation.

As you will see, your final Business Plan may end up as a simple summary, but the thought process involved in getting to simple is often a journey in itself!

* * *

Example 1: A.N.Author

PART 1: BUSINESS SUMMARY

Company Structure: Not necessary at the moment.

Business (or author) summary: A.N. Author writes epic fantasy novels.

Business goal/s: Make US$10,000 per year profit from book sales alone in the next three years.

Author brand: A.N. Author's epic fantasy novels feature dragons. Images of dragons will be used on the covers and the author website, and the color palette and theme will be imaginative and playful.

Genre/category and subcategories: Fantasy – Dragons & Mythical Creatures; Fantasy – Coming of Age; Fantasy – Epic (although this category is full of big-name traditionally published authors so it is very competitive).

Comparison authors: Lindsay Buroker's Agents of the Crown series

Reader avatar: People who read fantasy and in particular, have read and/or watched Game of Thrones. They also like Dungeons and Dragons, so might enjoy Stranger Things on Netflix. They like visual images, tattoos, gifts, etc., that feature dragons.

PART 2: PRODUCTION

Products: First novel in Dragon series completed and on Amazon in ebook and paperback. Second in series currently in first draft.

Although merchandise would be great fun, it's not something to pursue at this time. No other products or services and no desire to create anything other than books.

Writing process: Full-time at day job with no intention to leave. Writing process is currently 45 minutes spent dictating in the car before the kids are up three times a week.

Action Step: In order to work toward the business goal, add two more writing sessions per week and find a quiet place for editing.

Production schedule: Finish first draft of book 2 in the next six months; start drafting book 3. Three hours per week might not be enough.

Action Step: Review how I'm spending my time to find some extra hours.

Publishing and licensing strategy: One novel on Kindle Unlimited with the intention of publishing wide once there are three novels and a boxset completed.

Pricing strategy: US$4.99. Five free days per KU period

PART 3: MARKETING

Author ecosystem: Primarily centered around Amazon as the sales site. Pinterest Boards with dragon pictures.

Action Step: Allocate time for research on what aspects of marketing might work best for these books.

Author website: Currently have a free website on WordPress.com with an About page and book details. No time to expand this currently.

Email list and ARC team: Nothing currently.

Action Step: Take a tutorial and set this up so I have some readers for the next book.

Content marketing: Nothing currently. No time to expand this currently.

Paid advertising: FreeBooksy every 90 days to promote KU free days. This works well so keep doing this. Tried Amazon Ads but it was frustrating to use and there's no time to do this as well as write. Revisit next year once I have another book.

Social media: Pinterest Boards with dragon pictures. I enjoy this and it does seem to lead to clicks.

Action Step: Set up a Facebook Author Page so it's separate to my personal profile.

Author network: Nothing currently but I need this. *Action Step:* Investigate SFWA and author groups on Facebook.

PART 4: FINANCIALS

Money mindset: I know that fantasy authors can absolutely make money from their books. I intend to be one of them but I know it takes time. I've proven to myself that I can make a small amount from one book, so it must be possible to make more. I have doubts that it could ever outweigh my day job income, but since I have no intention of leaving, it doesn't matter at the moment. It's all extra.

Revenue model and income: Book sales and pages read from Amazon stores, paid monthly into bank account. Not much at the moment.

Initial investment and ongoing costs: Costs currently far outweigh any income. Not tracking this separately right now.

Action Step: Set up a separate bank account for my book income and expenses.

Paying yourself first and long-term investing: Not doing this currently. Will review at year three.

Next review date: Six months' time

* * *

Example 2: M.K. Author

PART 1: BUSINESS SUMMARY

Company Structure: Currently reporting my book and speaking income as part of my annual tax return as a sole trader.

Action Step: Find out the appropriate threshold for starting a company as incorporating will provide more efficient financials.

Business (or author) summary: M.K. Author helps mid-life professionals to transition into a new career with books, workshops, and consulting.

Business goal/s: Make US$50,000 per year profit from book sales and services (double what I currently make).

Author brand: M.K. Author offers no-nonsense and practical advice for career change. Non-fiction book covers feature large, clear text with a color palette of deeper blues for more authority. The same design elements are reflected on the website.

Genre/category and subcategories: Self-help-Personal Transformation; Happiness; Motivational; Business & Money – Career Guides

Comparison authors: Cal Newport; James Clear; Cassandra Gaisford.

Action Step: Consider how I could also appeal to fans of more inspirational speakers like Brené Brown.

Reader/customer avatar: Women over 45 whose children are not so dependent anymore, who are ready to focus more on themselves and step into their new career. They listen to podcasts like Women in the Middle: Loving Life After 50. Their guilty pleasures include Selling Sunset on Netflix.

PART 2: PRODUCTION

Products: Six career change books and one personal memoir, all in ebook and paperback (POD).

Action Step: Consider whether my memoir fits my brand. Options include changing the author name and separating it out completely, or possibly offering a class on writing a memoir since many mid-lifers are interested in this. It would also help me appeal to that more inspirational self-help market.

Action Step: Record (or outsource) audiobook editions and create workbooks.

Services: Live workshops running twice a year. In-person event turned into an online summit during the pandemic so I know it's possible.

Action Step: Turn the workshop into an evergreen course. Consider offering consulting one-on-one as a higher-priced service.

Writing process: Currently using a focused approach, blocking out several weeks with no meetings and few interruptions to complete the first draft. This is working well.

Production schedule: I don't need any more books, I need to make more of what I have. Focus on turning current assets into more streams of income in order to increase revenue.

Publishing and licensing strategy: Currently self-publishing on all ebook stores. Using KDP Print for paperbacks.

Action Step: Expand print distribution to Ingram Spark, enabling discounts for bookstores and easier bulk purchase.

Pricing strategy: US$7.99 for ebooks, no boxsets at the moment. Will need to consider if that's possible given the cap on ebook boxsets at Amazon.

PART 3: MARKETING

Author ecosystem: Main website MKAuthor.page is the hub for my books and services. LinkedIn as main social media with a Facebook Page for advertising, which I have only used for local event marketing.

Author website: Main website MKAuthor.page is the hub for my books and services.

Action Step: The author brand name is not big enough for what I want to achieve with the wider business. Consider a brand site for mid-lifers that is not my name. Keep the author name site and redirect to the Book page.

Email list and ARC team: Small email list, mainly focused on local market.

Action Step: Look at how I can build my email list to a wider market so I can sell globally.

Content marketing: Currently writing articles on my own site and guest posting on other mid-lifer sites.

Action Step: Pitch for podcast interviews on mid-life shows. Send five pitch emails per month.

Paid advertising: Currently using paid Facebook Ads for local market.

Action Step: Expand this for email list growth and also try for direct book sales.

Social media: Posting articles on LinkedIn. Facebook Business Page but not active there. Ads only.

Action Step: Make more of LinkedIn. Research the latest tools and ways to optimize my brand there.

Author network: Women's business network meetings in person in my city.

Action Step: Research online women's business groups to expand learning to global market rather than just local sales.

PART 4: FINANCIALS

Money mindset: I still have issues around self-worth and my lack of knowledge about money sometimes makes me feel stupid.

Action Step: Read financial books and learn the language.

Revenue model and income: Currently 50% revenue from book sales and 50% from live workshops.

Action Step: Make more of what I have! Expand books into audio-books, workbooks, and possibly boxsets. Look into affiliate revenue to make more of my website, email list, and books. Look at best options for online course hosting and start with something small. I am clearly leaving so much on the table!

Initial investment and ongoing costs: Current ongoing costs include website hosting, email list service, advertising for local events.

Action Step: I don't have enough time to do everything. Research out-sourcing to a virtual assistant for helping with advertising and maybe pitching podcasts. Start with ten hours a month and see if I can justify more over time.

Paying yourself first and long-term investing: Currently reinvest-ing all profits into the business and living off savings.

Action Step: Start paying myself a small amount every month on the same day and also investing the same amount. Start with $200 and review over time. I have to get started on this sometime. It might as well be now.

Next review date: Six months' time

* * *

These example Business Plans should give you some ideas for your own. Of course, you might have pages of other thoughts and answers to the deeper questions, but you can see how these summary sections quickly encapsulate where these authors are now and give some indi-cation of a future direction.

Your Author Business Plan

Date: _____

PART 1: BUSINESS SUMMARY

Company structure:

_____

_____

_____

_____

Business (or author) summary:

_____

_____

_____

_____

_____

_____

_____

Business goal/s:

_____

_____

_____

_____

_____

_____

_____

_____

_____

_____

_____

_____

_____

_____

_____

_____

_____

_____

Author brand:

Genre/category and subcategories:

_____

_____

_____

_____

_____

_____

Comparison authors:

_____

_____

_____

_____

_____

_____

_____

_____

_____

_____

_____

Reader avatar/s:

_____

_____

_____

_____

_____

_____

_____

_____

_____

_____

_____

_____

_____

_____

_____

_____

_____

_____

_____

_____

PART 2: PRODUCTION

Books/Products/Services:

_____

_____

_____

_____

_____

_____

_____

_____

_____

_____

_____

_____

_____

_____

_____

_____

_____

_____

Writing process:

_____

_____

_____

_____

_____

_____

_____

_____

_____

_____

_____

_____

_____

_____

_____

_____

_____

_____

_____

Production schedule:

_____

_____

_____

_____

_____

_____

_____

_____

_____

_____

_____

_____

_____

_____

_____

_____

_____

_____

Publishing and licensing strategy:

Pricing strategy:

PART 3: MARKETING

Author ecosystem:

_____

_____

_____

_____

_____

_____

_____

Author website:

_____

_____

_____

_____

_____

_____

_____

_____

_____

Email list and ARC team:

Content marketing:

_____

_____

_____

_____

_____

_____

_____

_____

Paid advertising:

_____

_____

_____

_____

_____

_____

_____

_____

_____

Social media:

_____

_____

_____

_____

_____

_____

_____

_____

Author network:

_____

_____

_____

_____

_____

_____

_____

_____

_____

_____

PART 4: FINANCIALS

Money mindset:

_____

_____

_____

_____

_____

_____

_____

_____

_____

_____

_____

_____

_____

_____

_____

_____

_____

_____

_____

Revenue model and income:

_____

_____

_____

_____

_____

_____

_____

_____

_____

_____

_____

_____

_____

_____

_____

_____

_____

_____

Initial investment and ongoing costs:

_____

_____

_____

_____

_____

_____

_____

_____

_____

_____

_____

_____

_____

_____

_____

_____

_____

_____

_____

_____

Paying yourself first and long-term investing:

_____

_____

_____

_____

_____

_____

_____

_____

_____

_____

_____

_____

_____

_____

Next review date:

_____

Conclusion

Congratulations!

You now have a finished Author Business Plan, a tool to help you navigate the journey ahead, wherever you're starting from right now, and a way to shape your creative future.

I wish you all the best on your author journey and happy writing!

Remember, you can find templates and more resources at:

www.TheCreativePenn.com/yourplan

Need more help on your author journey?

Sign up for my *free* Author 2.0 Blueprint and email series, and receive useful information on writing, publishing, book marketing, and making a living with your writing:

www.TheCreativePenn.com/blueprint

* * *

Love podcasts? Join me every Monday for The Creative Penn Podcast where I talk about writing, publishing, book marketing and the author business. Available on your favorite podcast app.

Find the backlist episodes at:

www.TheCreativePenn.com/podcast

Appendix 1: Resources

PART 1: BUSINESS SUMMARY

- *Creating Your Author Brand* – Kristine Kathryn Rusch

- Interview with Kristine Kathryn Rusch on Author Branding: www.TheCreativePenn.com/branding1

- Interview with Gail Carriger on Author Branding: www.TheCreativePenn.com/gail

- Brand Manual example – www.TheCreativePenn.com/yourplan

- Publisher Rocket, an investigative tool for finding the best categories and keywords: www.TheCreativePenn.com/rocket

- Specific genre reports at K-lytics: www.TheCreativePenn.com/genre

PART 2: PRODUCTION

- How to make a boxset – www.TheCreativePenn.com/create-boxset

- How to make a workbook edition – www.TheCreativePenn.com/create-workbook

- How to make Large Print editions – www.TheCreativePenn.com/large-print

- How to use software like Vellum or ProWritingAid, how to build your own website, or find and work with editors and book cover designers – www.TheCreativePenn.com/tools

- *Turn What You Know Into An Online Course.* You can find this and all my courses at www.TheCreativePenn.com/courses

- Reedsy, a marketplace for professional freelancers who work with authors www.TheCreativePenn.com/reedsy

- *Successful Self-Publishing: How to Self-Publish and Market Your Book* – Joanna Penn

- Wide for the Win Facebook Group for specific tips on publishing and marketing beyond just Amazon

- *How Authors Sell Publishing Rights: Sell your Book to Film, TV, Translation, and Other Rights Buyers* – Orna Ross and Helen Sedwick

- *Closing the Deal on Your Terms: Agents, Contracts, and Other Considerations* – Kristine Kathryn Rusch

- *Rethinking the Writing Business* – Kristine Kathryn Rusch

- *Hollywood vs the Author* – edited by Stephen Jay Schwartz

PART 3: MARKETING

- My tutorial on website hosting, design, and email setup: www.TheCreativePenn.com/authorwebsite

- Mini-course on *Content Marketing for Fiction*: www.TheCreativePenn.com/learn

- ConvertKit, the email service I use and recommend: www.TheCreativePenn.com/convert

- Tutorial on how to set up your email list with ConvertKit: www.TheCreativePenn.com/setup-email-list/

- Free webinar on data protection rules, privacy policy and more: www.TheCreativePenn.com/gdprhelp

- *Newsletter Ninja: How to Become an Author Mailing List Expert* – Tammi Labrecque

- *Rock-Solid Newsletter: How to Grow a Successful List of Devoted and Enthusiastic Readers* – Andrea Pearson

- *Do Open: How a Simple Email Newsletter Can Transform Your Business* – David Hieatt

- *Content Marketing for Fiction* – course by Joanna Penn www.TheCreativePenn.com/courses

- *Master Content Marketing: A Simple Strategy To Cure The Blank Page Blues and Attract a Profitable Audience* – Pamela Wilson

- *Master Content Strategy: How to Maximise your Reach and Boost your Bottom Line Every Time You Hit Publish* – Pamela Wilson

- *Content 10X: More Content, Less Time, Maximum Results* – Amy Woods

- List of free and paid promotion sites: Kindlepreneur.com/list-sites-promote-free-amazon-books

- *Advertising for Authors* course by Mark Dawson: www.TheCreativePenn.com/ads

- BookBub Insights blog: insights.bookbub.com

- *BookBub Ads Expert: A Marketing Guide to Author Discovery* – David Gaughran

- *Ads for Authors Who Hate Math* – Chris Fox

- Printable calendar pages: www.calendarpedia.co.uk

- Social media scheduling: Buffer.com

- *Networking for Authors: How to Make Friends, Sell More Books, and Grow a Publishing Network from Scratch* – Dan Parsons

- Interview on Networking for Authors with Dan Parsons – www.TheCreativePenn.com/networking

PART 4: FINANCIALS

- List of recommended books and podcasts about money: www.TheCreativePenn.com/moneybooks

- Financial management software: Xero.com

Appendix 2: Bibliography

Closing the Deal on Your Terms: Agents, Contracts, and Other Considerations – Kristine Kathryn Rusch

Content 10X: More Content, Less Time, Maximum Results – Amy Woods

Creating Your Author Brand – Kristine Kathryn Rusch

Do Open: How a Simple Email Newsletter Can Transform Your Business – David Hieatt

Hollywood vs the Author – edited by Stephen Jay Schwartz

How to Market a Book – Joanna Penn

How Authors Sell Publishing Rights: Sell your Book to Film, TV, Translation, and Other Rights Buyers – Orna Ross and Helen Sedwick

Master Content Marketing: A Simple Strategy To Cure The Blank Page Blues and Attract a Profitable Audience – Pamela Wilson

Master Content Strategy: How to Maximise your Reach and Boost your Bottom Line Every Time You Hit Publish – Pamela Wilson

Money Book List: www.TheCreativePenn.com/moneybooks

Networking for Authors: How to Make Friends, Sell More Books, and Grow a Publishing Network from Scratch – Dan Parsons

Newsletter Ninja: How to Become an Author Mailing List Expert – Tammi Labrecque

Productivity for Authors: Find Time to Write, Organize your Author Life, and Decide What Really Matters – Joanna Penn

Rethinking the Writing Business – Kristine Kathryn Rusch

Rock-Solid Newsletter: How to Grow a Successful List of Devoted and Enthusiastic Readers – Andrea Pearson

Successful Self-Publishing: How to Self-Publish and Market Your Book – Joanna Penn

About Joanna Penn

Joanna Penn, writing as J.F.Penn, is an award-nominated, New York Times and USA Today bestselling author of thrillers and dark fantasy, as well as writing inspirational non-fiction for authors.

She is an international professional speaker, podcaster, and award-winning entrepreneur. She lives in Bath, England with her husband and enjoys a nice G&T.

Joanna's award-winning site for writers, TheCreativePenn.com, helps people to write, publish and market their books through articles, audio, video and online products as well as live workshops.

Love thrillers? www.JFPenn.com

Love travel? www.BooksAndTravel.page

Connect with Joanna
www.TheCreativePenn.com
joanna@TheCreativePenn.com

www.twitter.com/thecreativepenn
www.facebook.com/TheCreativePenn
www.Instagram.com/jfpennauthor
www.youtube.com/thecreativepenn

More Books and Courses from Joanna Penn

Non-Fiction Books for Authors

How to Write Non-Fiction

How to Market a Book

How to Make a Living with your Writing

Productivity for Authors

Successful Self-Publishing

Your Author Business Plan

The Successful Author Mindset

Public Speaking for Authors,
Creatives and Other Introverts

Audio for Authors:
Audiobooks, Podcasting, and Voice Technologies

The Healthy Writer

Business for Authors: How to be an Author Entrepreneur

Career Change

www.TheCreativePenn.com/books

Courses for Authors

How to Write a Novel

How to Write Non-Fiction

Multiple Streams of Income from your Writing

Your Author Business Plan

Content Marketing for Fiction

Productivity for Authors

Turn What You Know Into An Online Course

Co-Writing a Book

www.TheCreativePenn.com/courses

***

Thriller and Dark Fantasy Novels as J.F.Penn

ARKANE Action-adventure Thrillers

Stone of Fire #1
Crypt of Bone #2
Ark of Blood #3
One Day in Budapest #4
Day of the Vikings #5
Gates of Hell #6
One Day in New York #7
Destroyer of Worlds #8
End of Days #9
Valley of Dry Bones #10
Tree of Life #11

Brooke and Daniel Crime Thrillers

Desecration #1
Delirium #2
Deviance #3

Mapwalker Dark Fantasy Trilogy

Map of Shadows #1
Map of Plagues #2
Map of the Impossible #3

Other books and short stories

Risen Gods

A Thousand Fiendish Angels

The Dark Queen

More books coming soon.

Get your free thriller at:
www.JFPenn.com/free